EASY
TO BELIEVE

John Davis Hendricks

Christian Research and Fellowship
P.O. Box 670853
Marietta, Georgia 30066

All Bible quotations are from
the King James Version
unless otherwise noted.

Printed in the USA by Morris Publishing
3212 East Highway 30 • Kearney, NE 68847 • 1-800-650-7888

Biblical Studies Available
by Reverend John Hendricks
Include:

Books: *Prosperity God's Way*
                    Easy to Believe
                    God's Healing Word
                    Power From On High

Audio CDs: Teachings on Many Subjects
                    (Request a list.)

Seminars: *Prosperity God's Way*
                    Renewed Unto Love
                    Sonship
                    The Living Hope

Classes: Foundational Class
                        (*To Know God*)
                    Advanced Class on
                    the Nine Manifestations
                        (*To Know God*)

Write to:

Christian Research and Fellowship
P.O. Box 670853
Marietta, GA 30066

To my daughter

Rochelle Leigh Hendricks

Who worked with the same
dedication and effort
that I did
and skipped a semester of college
in order to complete this book

CONTENTS

Introduction

The law of believing is the most important truth and principle in a person's life. Nothing determines our lives upon earth, their successes and failures, nearly as powerfully as the law of believing. It is the basic principle to gain control of your life, to be a successful person, to be a successful Christian, and to live a life of victorious freedom. The law of believing is how we appropriate eternal life and is one of the main factors in acquiring eternal rewards. It must be understood in order for a Christian to know God, to live for God, to enjoy God, and to receive His blessings.

We are not attempting to cover in entirety everything about the law of believing in this biblical study, but we will cover it thoroughly enough to give you a sure biblical footing, an accurate foundation to build upon, to grow in, and especially to achieve numerous successes in your power-filled walk with God.

CHAPTER 1

The Principle of Believing

The principle of believing or the law of believing is a truth from God's Word; it is the Truth of God's Word. Actually, to call it a law is an understatement; for scientific laws such as gravity can be broken or defied, but a truth from God's Word cannot ever be broken or defied. Certainly someone can operate an opposing principle to defy gravity. A simple example is a missile or a rocket soaring upward rather than being tugged to the ground by the earth's gravitational pull. A truth from God's Word can never, ever be defied or broken.

Matthew 5:18:
For verily I say unto you, Till heaven and earth pass, one jot or one tittle shall in no wise pass from the law, till all be fulfilled.

This principle, the truth of believing, has never been broken or altered since the dawn of time and never will be.

1

The law of believing is literally your rudder in life. A ship's rudder guides it and, in time, will navigate the ship to its desired location. As you learn to **simply** operate the principle of believing, it will be to your life as a ship's rudder and take you to your desired destinations. A ship in the sea has many factors affecting it (waves, winds, and currents), and the rudder is constantly being moved about to direct the ship to its desired location. There are many factors pulling, pushing, and tugging at you, but it is this truth of believing from God's Word that will determine where you end up and whether you succeed or fail in every endeavor.

In simple essence, what you **expect** to happen will happen. What you truly expect will come to pass in your life. Certainly, there are limitations and other influences, which we will examine later. Another simple way to state it is what a person confesses in his heart is going to happen in his life and what a person thinks of himself determines who he is. In other words, **if you really believe something in your heart, it will come to pass, and what you really believe in your heart about yourself is what you are in life.** You are who you believe you are.

Proverbs 23:7a:
For as he thinketh in his heart, so is he...

You will go in life exactly where you believe to go. If you learn from God's Word how to believe rightly, you can **change to become the person you desire to be** and you can change your life to achieve anything **you want to achieve**. With this principle of believing, you can gain control of your life and reach your desired destinations, no matter how contrary the winds and currents are.

Mark 9:23:
Jesus said unto him, If thou canst believe, all things are possible to him that believeth.

This verse shows the limitlessness of what you can do when you learn to believe God's Word.

We are embarking on a study in God's true Word that could change you in a dynamic and exciting way, giving you a new life filled with victories and successes in every facet.

Romans 8:37:
Nay, in all these things we are more than conquerors through him that loved us.

You can, with God's Word and God's help, **overcome everything** that has ever held you back by believing and trusting God.

There are two biblical synonyms for believing. In the Old Testament the word used for believing God is "**trust**." To trust God is to believe God. In the New Testament another word, "**confidence**," is used for believing. To have confidence in God is to believe God. To have confidence in yourself is to believe in yourself. In this biblical study, trusting God will be used many times, which is exactly the same as believing God or having confidence in God. These are all equal to each other and have the same meaning. In our day and time, the word "trust" is commonly used and easily understood; therefore, using this word will make it easier to understand the principle of believing.

Believing works so simply as shown in Mark 11:23:

> For verily I say unto you, That whosoever shall say unto this mountain, Be thou removed, and be thou cast into the sea; and shall not doubt in his heart, but shall believe that those things which he saith shall come to pass; he shall have whatsoever he saith.

It says "whosoever." This displays God's love for all people and how He is no respecter of persons.* The law of believing does work for anyone—"whosoever."

"...Shall say...." This is very important. You must confess it, say it, in your heart. Jesus Christ used the mountain to represent the impossible. Causing a great mountain to be cast into the sea by saying it in your heart is in the realm of the miraculous.

"And shall not doubt in his heart...." The word "heart" is *kardia* in Greek and its meaning is the innermost being, not just the mind which perceives and thinks many thoughts, but our hearts. Later, we will examine how believing proceeds from the heart. The following explains how the principle of believing operates:

- The person says it in his heart,
- does not doubt,
- believes what he says in his heart,
- then whatever he said comes to pass.

When you trust God, you have no doubt. When you trust God to bring something to pass, you are believing.

---

*Romans 2:11: For there is no respect of persons with God.

5

Verse 24:
Therefore I say unto you, What things soever ye desire, when ye pray, believe that ye receive them, and ye shall have them.

Look at how simple this is: pray and expect the things you desire to happen (believe), and you shall have them. How easy. This is why little children receive so many answers to their prayers and perform many miracles.

Someone who is not born again can receive healings and miracles in his life by believing. In this situation, God has to bring a person around who is born again of His spirit to perform the healing or miracle.[*] This does occur with a level of frequency and often opens the hearts of the un-born again ones to receive the new birth.

You are in life where your believing has taken you, and you are who you believe you are. We just read how you can receive answers to all your prayers, you can go **where you want to go** by believing and trusting God, and you can be **whom you want to be** by trusting and believing

---

[*]For a true miracle or healing from God to be performed, a three-part man, one born again of God's spirit, must perform the miracle. The miracle is a manifestation of the spirit in one of God's children. To understand this more fully, you can attend the yearly advanced classes.

God. You should work this biblical study in your heart to the point that it is commonplace for your prayers to be answered. God loves you, He is your Father, and He desires to answer your prayers more than you desire to have them answered. As you develop your trust in God, more and more of your prayers will be answered and you will learn to bring to pass the impossible, the miraculous, consistently. **Say it in your heart, trust God to bring it to pass, and you will have whatsoever you said.** This is the simplicity of the law of believing.

Let's study an account of two people who trusted God in the direst of situations.

Mark 5:22 and 23:
And, behold, there cometh one of the rulers of the synagogue, Jairus by name; and when he saw him [Jesus], he fell at his feet,

And besought him greatly, saying, My little daughter lieth at the point of death: I pray thee, come and lay thy hands on her, that she may* be healed; and she shall live.

---

*There is no corresponding Greek word for "may" in verse 23 in any Greek text. It is added and other translations render the phrase: "so that she will be healed and live."

In verse 23 we saw that Jairus greatly besought Jesus. One thing to note is that "believe" is a verb and when someone believes, he **acts upon his belief**. Jairus believed that Jesus the Christ could heal his daughter and save her life; therefore, he came to him. The proof someone is really believing in his heart is that he **acts upon his beliefs**. Jairus did not sit at home mourning the soon-coming death of his daughter. Instead, he believed and trusted God; therefore, he went to Jesus and besought him greatly. He acted on what he believed, which is the proof he believed it in his heart. And then he said with the conviction of his heart, "So that she will be healed and live." Look at his confession, what he is saying. This shows his trust in God. He was believing for his daughter to be delivered from death.

Verses 24—26:
And Jesus went with him; and much people followed him, and thronged him.

And a certain woman, which had an issue of blood twelve years,

And had suffered many things of many physicians, and had spent all that she had, and was nothing bettered, but rather grew worse,

8

Verses 27 and 28:
When she had heard of Jesus, came in the press behind, and touched his garment.

For she said, If I may touch but his clothes, I shall be whole.

Look at what this woman said in her heart in verse 28. Look at what she believed in her heart. Her confession was that if she could just touch Jesus Christ's clothes, she would be made whole. She said, "I shall be whole."

We are seeing two people in two of life's most tragic and heart-rending situations. The man is facing the death of his daughter, and this wonderful woman has been robbed of her finances and health to the point of great suffering and misery, yet in their hearts both are **expecting the impossible to come to pass**. They are expecting complete deliverance.

Matthew 9:21:
For she said within[*] herself, If I may but touch his garment, I shall be whole.

---

[*]Jairus made his confession out loud before all, and the woman made her confession within. Both believed in their hearts and received.

This verse from Matthew shows that you can say things within yourself, as other verses convey that you can say things out loud. It makes no difference; it is just important that you trust God in your heart to bring it to pass. If this wonderful woman could believe God to be delivered from her terrible condition, then anyone can be delivered of anything. This account clearly depicts the simplicity and the accuracy of the law of believing.

Mark 5:29—31:
And straightway the fountain of her blood was dried up; and she felt in her body that she was healed of that plague.

And Jesus, immediately knowing in himself that virtue had gone out of him, turned him about in the press, and said, Who touched my clothes?

And his disciples said unto him, Thou seest the multitude thronging thee, and sayest thou, Who touched me?

Look at the great believing of this woman. She did not even need to be prayed for or to speak with Jesus Christ; she just touched his clothing. Then God showed Jesus that the power of a miracle had gone out of him. When he asked his disciples about being touched, they were no help, but he, walking with God, sought out the woman.

Verses 32—34:
And he looked round about to see her that had done this thing.

But the woman fearing and trembling, knowing what was done in her, came and fell down before him, and told him all the truth.

And he said unto her, Daughter, thy faith [believing]* hath made thee whole; go in peace, and be whole of thy plague.

After he sought her out and she came to him, in verse 34 he encouraged her to be strong in her trust and to stay healed. Sometimes when people are delivered, they need to be encouraged to stand firm on the Word or they can lose their deliverance. Jesus Christ was encouraging and establishing the healing for her. This is the love and encouragement that people need in order to be established in the Word. Some of you must

---

*The Greek word *pistis* is translated "believing" in the King James Version and is also translated "faith." Here it should be translated "believing," just as it is many other times. This wrong translating of *pistis* into "faith" has become a confusing, nebulous doctrine in many religious circles.

11

rise up to encourage others in God's Word and to help establish them so they can be delivered and stay delivered.

Verse 35:
While he yet spake, there came from the ruler of the synagogue's house certain which said, Thy daughter is dead: why troublest thou the Master any further?

In verse 35 Jairus the ruler is believing, but he is confronted with the ultimate negative, the ultimate discouragement. Many times people are believing when other people and situations come at them to tear down their trust so they do not succeed. However, in this account, Jesus Christ retaliated with the positive words of truth.

Verse 36:
As soon as Jesus heard the word that was spoken, he saith unto the ruler of the synagogue, Be not afraid, only believe.

When the ruler was confronted with the death of his daughter, Jesus Christ immediately (before the ruler could fall apart mentally and emotionally, thus the trust in his heart be broken) spoke the words, "Be not afraid, only believe." These are the words you must hide in your heart. "Be not afraid, only trust." No matter how dire, no matter how wicked, no matter how discouraging the situation looks, do not let anything or anyone talk you into being afraid. Trust God, believe Him, and whatever you say in your heart He, God, will bring to pass.

Verses 37—40:
And he suffered no man to follow him, save Peter, and James, and John the brother of James.

And he cometh to the house of the ruler of the synagogue, and seeth the tumult, and them that wept and wailed greatly.

And when he was come in, he saith unto them, Why make ye this ado, and weep? the damsel is not dead, but sleepeth.

And they laughed him to scorn. But when he had put them all out, he taketh the father and the mother of the damsel, and them that were with him, and entereth in where the damsel was lying.

Jesus Christ could not have put the scoffers and the laughers out of the house had not Jairus consented and agreed. Jairus believed that his daughter would be raised from the dead; therefore, he **acted** as Jesus desired.

13

Verses 41—43:
And he took the damsel by the hand, and said unto her, Talitha cumi; which is, being interpreted, Damsel, I say unto thee, arise.

And straightway the damsel arose, and walked; for she was of the age of twelve years. And they were astonished with a great astonishment.

And he charged them straitly that no man should know it; and commanded that something should be given her to eat.

We just read in the Word of God about a woman who was at the end of her rope physically and financially, but she believed, confessing in her heart that if she touched Jesus' garment, she would be healed. She acted, which is the proof she was trusting in her heart (for what one truly believes one will act upon), and she received her full deliverance.

We also read about Jairus who was tempted to have a broken heart, but instead he stayed positive, trusting God. The proof that he trusted God was his action. He went to Jesus and said in front of all, "Master, you pray for my daughter and she will live." This man remained adamantly trusting God even though his daughter died before they arrived to pray for her.

These are examples of how you can be adamantly adamant on the promises of God's Word in any situation and receive God's miraculous deliverance. These last two examples from the Word of God were dealing with the most difficult situations. However, there will be thousands of smaller situations that you can and will believe God to change and improve by a confident word of prayer.

CHAPTER 2

Easy To Believe

A very important truth the child of God must keep **fresh** in his heart is that believing is **easy**. To trust God is to believe God. Little children are born with an innate trust. You can throw a very small child in the air and catch him over and over again, and he will be completely at ease, trusting you to catch him. However, as he grows older, takes a few spills, and his parents tell him one thing and do another, he learns distrust and even fear. Sometimes young children who know the Bible display a very pure courage and trust in God, even in the most difficult situations. Well into the hundreds of times, parents have told me that during trying situations in which they had become discouraged, losing heart, their small child (whom they had taught the Word of God) spoke the pure, simple positives of trusting God. The children caused their parents to encourage themselves in God and regain their confidence.

God designed you to trust and believe Him, but the world and the people in it are constantly gnawing and grinding on the purity of your trust.

Proverbs 3:5 and 6:
Trust in the LORD with all thine heart; and lean not unto thine own understanding.

In all thy ways acknowledge him, and he shall direct thy paths.

It says to trust in God. The word "Lord" is *Jehovah*, meaning God in His covenant relationship, the One who fulfills His promises. Trust in Him with **all** your heart. This is God's will and God's Word for you, to trust Him with all your heart. Trusting God will cause you to have great successes and great victories.

At times, people trust God in several places, but not in others. However, we want to develop God's Word in our hearts to trust God in every phase and facet of our lives in order that we trust Him with our whole hearts.

Then it says, "...lean not unto thine own understanding." This is the great enemy of believing or trust. Nothing will cause you to fall short more in your trust (believing) walk with

God than to lean to your own understanding. People try to figure out what other people are thinking and how they will react. They try to figure out the future. They try to figure out how to behave in order to succeed. This will reap failure and misery for the child of God, hindering his relationship with God. There is such peace and stability in trusting God with all your heart by not speculating about people, situations, and the future. Not once in all my years have I seen a person who leans to his own understanding, figuring everything out, have correct judgment with any consistency. It is nothing more than a mental spider web of anxiety and frustration—no way for the child of God to live.

"In all thy ways acknowledge him...." God is your Father; He desires to be your dearest friend. He fathered you to have someone to love and for **companionship**. The verse says to acknowledge Him in all your ways. In everything you do, you talk to Him, say a little prayer (don't make it formal), thank Him in all the little things and all the important things, too. Doing this will cause you to believe God for many, many victories.

"...And he shall direct thy paths." He will direct your paths by bringing the appropriate verses from His Word to your remembrance, by talking with you (revelation), and by inspiring others to speak what you need to hear.

To trust God is so very **simple**. Believing God is extremely **easy**. For instance, you have five dollars in your wallet. You take the five dollar bill out and decide to buy a Big Mac, fry, and drink. You are totally confident; you totally trust that the green, wrinkled piece of paper will enable you to purchase your hamburger. You have no anxiety, no worry or fear, just absolute trust in the not-so-trustworthy United States government that prints the money. That is believing; that is trust. You have full confidence and trust with all your heart that you can purchase the Big Mac and fry. You are not nervous about it; you do not have to fight off negative thoughts. You believe you can take that piece of paper and receive food for it, and you trust in it with all your heart. This proves it is very easy to believe. Although, it is possible (not probable, but possible) for something to go wrong and your purchase to fail. For example, a power outage could prevent the burgers from being cooked, or the cashier could take your five dollars and realize it is counterfeit money someone has slipped to you. It is certainly possible for you to have complications with your purchase.

The piece of paper in the Bible that contains the Truth of God's Word states the following in Philippians 4:19:

> But my God shall supply all your need according to his riches in glory by Christ Jesus.

This piece of paper is backed by the Creator, the true and faithful God, and has been around long before the U.S. government existed. It is absolutely impossible for God to forsake His promise. He will always fulfill His promise for a trusting son.

> Hebrews 6:18:
> ...it was impossible for God to lie, we might have a strong consolation...

> Titus 1:2:
> ...God, that cannot lie...

It is impossible for God to lie; God cannot lie. His Word is the Truth. You can and should stake your life on it. Our minds have been trained to trust in a fluctuating dollar backed by a corrupt, untrustworthy government. We can and we must learn God's Word and operate His power to **retrain our minds** to trust in the Almighty God. We can learn to trust Him beyond the dollar and McDonalds, to trust Him with all our hearts. It is not difficult, but you certainly need a strong desire to develop this trust in God.

Those of you who already speak in tongues can speak in tongues at any time, at any place, in any amount you desire. That is the faithfulness of our God. It is impossible for Him to ever let you down. And none of you have ever experienced one second when God was not there to inspire those words in your mind or out of your mouth.

Matthew 19:26:
But Jesus beheld them, and said unto them, With men this is impossible; but with God all things are possible.

There is absolutely nothing that is impossible for God. All things are possible to His children. **You can overcome anything.** No matter how deep the fear is, no matter how terrible the disease is, with God all certainly can be overcome. The sons of God must approach believing or trusting God not only as easy, but as something they are going to do, **adamantly refusing to accept any other train of thought**.

Philippians 4:13:
I can do all things through Christ which strengtheneth me.

You can trust God. You can believe God in the most adverse of situations because God has placed His spirit in you; therefore, you can gather your strength from within. **You can believe God. So not only is it easy to believe God, but you are also able to believe God.** You should become adamantly adamant that you are believing God. This is what is meant when it says, "...having done all, to stand," in Ephesians 6:13:

Wherefore take unto you the whole armour of God, that ye may be able to withstand in the evil day, and having **done all, to stand**.

You are like a great boulder; the winds, waves, and currents splash over you, go around you, and flow by you, yet you stand firm knowing that God is your Father and He will answer your prayers.

John 16:23:
And in that day ye shall ask me nothing. Verily, verily, I say unto you, Whatsoever ye shall ask the Father in my name, he will give it you.

CHAPTER 3

Right and Wrong Believing

There are two types or two sides of believing. The first side is right believing, believing correctly, which means to believe the doctrine of the Word of God. When what you believe in your heart is the Word of God or is harmonious with God's Word, you are believing correctly, or rightly. The other side is when something you believe is contrary to the Word of God or out of harmony with God's Word; then you are believing incorrectly, or wrongly. When Christians or non-Christians believe things that are contrary to the Word, they will receive negative results in their lives. But when the knowledgeable Christian believes the truths of God's Word, his life will be dynamically changed in a positive manner, thus receiving great positive results.

It is important to note that the unbeliever and the Christian who does not know God's Word only deal with positive and negative believing. Positive and negative believing certainly work exactly and precisely, but are a giant step beneath believing **the truths and promises of God's Word**.

Believing is a law. When one believes that negative things are going to happen, they will happen. When one believes that positive things will happen, they are going to happen. This law governs men's lives and works for Christian and non-Christian. However, the Christian who knows God's Word has a fabulous advantage: he can believe in the promises of God, operating the miraculous power of God to bring to pass the impossible. This truth that what a person believes in his heart will come into fruition in his life will explain many things that happen to people. It is the answer to the big "why" in life that people are always asking.

On the negative side of believing, there are three mental attitudes that defeat people. One of these is **doubt**. If you doubt in your heart that God will bless you, then you do not allow Him the privilege of blessing you. Secondly, and even worse, is **worry**. When you worry about negative things happening, it hampers your peace and relationship with God, as well as drawing the negatives to you. Worst of all is the believer's main enemy **fear**, the one thing that truly defeats God's children. When you fear negative results, you will surely receive those negatives in your life. Fear binds people, enslaves them, and is the root problem for most failure.

Fear[*] is the principal tool of the adversary, the primary way he defeats believers. Whatever believers or unbelievers fear they receive. No matter who you are, once you fear something in your heart, it is going to happen. Fear has defeated God's children more than all other evil combined. Fear is the opposite of believing and trusting God. When and where you have fear, you have wrong believing. At the place where fear is you will not receive the promises of God, but the agony and defeat of fear.

I John 4:18:
There is no fear in love; but perfect love casteth out fear: because fear hath torment. He that feareth is not made perfect in love.

---

[*]Whenever you see the word "fear" in the Bible, it is always used in one of two ways and the context will cause the meaning to be obvious. The first usage of the word "fear" means "respect and reverence" and is used many times of respect and reverence for God and occasionally for men of authority. The second way it is used is the usage we are commonly acquainted with in our day and time—the negative, binding fear which is wrong believing.

This great spiritual law of believing has governed men's lives since the dawn of time. For instance, if a person is afraid of cancer, he will receive it. Fear ties people up in knots; it defeats them. If a person is afraid of losing his job, he will lose his job.

During my adolescent years, there were many things in life that confounded me, perplexed me, and just seemed plain crazy. From my five senses point of view, life seemed to move in a random, illogical manner without purpose, without reason or rhyme. However, as I came to the great truths of God's Word, the opposite was true. There was no such thing as luck. There were specific principles that governed men's lives.

During those adolescent years, I had two friends. One's name was Tim; the other's was Barry. Tim became my friend because he allowed me to drive his new sportscar and taught me more about basketball. Tim had a very unique personality. He was obnoxious, cocky, and had the worst smart-aleck mouth of any person I had ever met. He took pleasure in offending and irritating everyone, making him many enemies. Tim was also a rather unattractive teenager with a very large nose, protruding front teeth, and a recessed chin.

One Saturday, I was driving Tim's car through a popular teenage hangout when Tim said, "John, pull over. I want to talk to that girl in the green car."

I glanced at the girl in the green car and then took a double-take. She was gorgeous. I thought to myself, "How can I tell Tim? He is very unattractive and his personality is obnoxious. He's just going to get his feelings hurt." Then cocky Tim began to brag about how he was a ladies' man, boasting that this girl would fall hopelessly in love with him. I chuckled to myself and thought, "He's going to get what he deserves."

So Tim strolled over, chatted with the girl for a while, and came back with a cocky grin on his face and a date for that night. However, I ended up with a giant question mark embedded in my brain.

Later, I developed a better friendship with a teenager named Barry. Barry was an all-around great guy and an all-around great friend. If you ever needed a ride, help, or money, you could count on Barry. There was one unusual thing about Barry; he was absolutely, even to this day, the most handsome male I have ever met. He was approximately 6'4" and in superb athletic condition—I mean superb! He had creamy olive skin, a chiseled angular face, large brown eyes, high cheekbones, and pencil-line eyebrows. I had not met too many people nicer than him, and no one more handsome.

One Thursday after school, Barry and I met at Pete's Pockets Billiards to play pool. As I was shooting at an eight ball, I noticed Barry slumping in the chair with a sad demeanor. I put my pool stick down, walked over, and sat in the chair next to him. I asked, "Hey, what's bugging you?"

He said, "I'm having problems with my girlfriend. I think she doesn't like me that much."

It was all I could do not to laugh. I thought to myself, "Barry, you could have any girl in the world, any one! And you're all upset about this girl I wouldn't even date!" Of course, I didn't say it because I was concerned it would offend him. So I just listened as he poured out more worry and anxiety about his relationship with his girlfriend.

Later, Barry's girlfriend dropped him. In fact, his next two girlfriends dropped him, too; and the last time I saw him, his wife had left him.

Can you imagine my confusion? Life seemed to be operating in a backwards manner, opposite of any reasoning. Why?

To make matters more perplexing, I learned that Tim had several very attractive girlfriends and the very girl he met at the hangout ended up being in love with him.

Why? I will tell you why. Because there is a principle or a law that governs all men's lives. It is the principle of believing. In simple essence, whatever a man or woman expects is what he or she gets. Stated another way, what one believes in one's heart, one receives. This is the greatest law in life. This is the greatest principle in God's Word. This is the greatest truth one can know.

Later in life, I became acquainted with two other gentlemen whose lives depicted this principle. One was David L. He was slightly retarded, but had numerous financial successes. The other acquaintance was Roger W. He was a very hard-working, exceedingly bright Harvard graduate with several degrees. Yet, he could not financially succeed to the point of providing for his family. Why? This great truth, the principle or law of believing, is exactly why: **what someone expects in his life he will receive**.

Tim believed positively that women would like him, and they were drawn to him because of his positive believing. Barry worried and feared, which are types of negative believing, and this destroyed his relationships with the opposite sex. David L. was simple and extremely positive and believed to prosper. Roger W. was full of anxiety, worry, and fear and believed negatively, which brought on his financial demise.

Let's examine some more scriptures about fear.

Job 3:25:
For the thing which I greatly feared is come upon me, and that which I was afraid of is come unto me.

This is exactly what happened to Job. He feared and brought calamity to himself: loss of wealth, loss of health, and loss of family. Later Job changed and broke his mental pattern of fear. After he began trusting God again, he regained two-fold all that he had lost.

Psalms 27:1:
The LORD is my light and my salvation; whom shall I fear? the LORD is the strength of my life; of whom shall I be afraid?

Verses 2 and 3:
When the wicked, even mine enemies and my foes, came upon me to eat up my flesh, they stumbled and fell.

Though an host should encamp against me, my heart shall not fear: though war should rise against me, in this will I be confident.

David wrote this psalm, and he literally lived this psalm. It was not just a beautiful writing, but his very life. David time and time again trusted God to take care of him in seemingly impossible situations. Later in life, David's believing in God's promise opened the door for God to give him the whole kingdom. **By believing God**, David took the kingdom of Israel to great heights.

Fear is wrong believing; it is the opposite of what God desires. It enslaves, captivates, and causes misery and failure. Doubt, worry, and fear are like a bad scrape on a person's leg. The scrape is slightly disabling and painful. If not taken care of properly, the scrape can become infected, which is more damaging and painful. Then it requires more work to treat the infection. If the infection is not properly taken care of, gangrene can set in, destroying the use of the leg.

The scrape is like doubt, the infection is like worry, and the gangrene is like fear. They work in the same progressive manner.

On the other hand, to have confidence in God is to believe God, to trust God is to believe God, and certainly to believe God is to believe God. All cause a person to reap the promises of God and the blessings of God.

In the following verses, Jesus Christ encouraged his disciples not to worry about being provided for.

Matthew 6:26 and 27:
Behold the fowls of the air: for they sow not, neither do they reap, nor gather into barns; yet your heavenly Father feedeth them. Are ye not much better than they?

Which of you by taking thought [anxiety filled thoughts] can add one cubit unto his stature?

How simple, how logical this is. No matter how much you worry or how hard you worry about it, you will not change your height one inch. Worry and concern add nothing to a person's life. They have never solved one problem. All they do is rob people of the peace and joy God intended for them to have. We must study God's Word and learn to operate the power of God in order to eliminate these negative thought patterns.

Proverbs 29:25:
The fear of man bringeth a snare...

Fear is binding; it is enslaving and defeating. The reason people have so much fear and worry is our culture with magazines, TV shows, etc. bombarding them constantly with negatives. The newscasters travel across the United States and even the world to hyperbolize negatives. They import every rape, murder, and sensational crime from all over the world to build worry and fear in our society. If you do not have seventy-two different kinds of insurance, your whole life and family are in constant jeopardy. The sales pitches of today constantly use fear to motivate people. If you do not take this vitamin, this pill, have these X-rays and this test, or eat this way, you will have all these terrible health problems. We are being fed a negative diet that is more poisonous and harmful to our hearts, minds, and bodies than junkfood could ever be. I am not suggesting that it is wrong to take good care of yourself; I am stating that the negativity and fear are very damaging, even more damaging than improper physical hygiene.

II Timothy 1:7:
For God hath not given us the spirit of fear;
but of power, and of love, and of a sound
mind.

II Timothy declares that God has not given
us the spirit of fear. We have power; we have
love; He has given us a sound mind. Love is
more healing than any medication, healthfood, or
physical therapy ever dreamed of being. We can
come to God and His Word and change our
negative mental diet to a positive feast of love,
joy, and peace. We can learn to trust God to
bring to pass miracles of goodness, healing, and
financial freedom to our lives. Only you can
discipline your mental intake, what you think
about, in order to live this life of trusting God. It
is your decision.

With God's Word and God's power you can
be free from all worries and fears.

Psalm 34:4:
I sought the LORD[*] [God], and he heard me,
and delivered me from all my fears.

---

[*]The Hebrew word used here is *Jehovah*, which means God in His
covenant relationship to man.

David said, "...he...delivered me from **all** my fears." People have financial fears; they have fears about their health; they have fears about the future; they have worries about their children; they have fears in their relationships with others. But David said that he sought the Lord and He delivered him from all his fears. We can be worry-free and fear-free by going to God's Word and operating His power.

After exposing the number one enemy of God's people and mankind, we need to study the **how** of eradicating fear in our lives. In order to be free, joy-filled successes as sons of God, we must learn how to keep ourselves free from fear and **on guard** to the temptation of fear. Fear is always wrong; it is wrong believing. It is the number one cause of failure in any segment of life.

I John 4:18:
There is no fear in love; but perfect love casteth out fear: because fear hath torment. He that feareth is not made perfect in love.

Fear is mentally tormenting, but perfect love casts out fear, eliminates all fear from your life.

37

Let's delve into someone's life who was defeated by fear, then later changed, developing this perfect love to become absolutely fearless.

Peter had vehemently argued with Jesus Christ that he would stand beside him and go with him to the very death. Jesus Christ warned Peter that he would not have the courage to carry through with his words and would deny him. Peter really meant what he said with all his heart. He was adamantly committed to it, but as we read these verses, you will see fear beat Peter down into failure.

Luke 22:54—57:
Then took they him [Jesus Christ], and led him, and brought him into the high priest's house. And Peter followed afar off.

And when they had kindled a fire in the midst of the hall, and were set down together, Peter sat down among them.

But a certain maid beheld him as he sat by the fire, and earnestly looked upon him, and said, This man was also with him.

And he denied him, saying, Woman, I know him not.

Peter denied even knowing Jesus Christ. It had not quite dawned on him that he was behaving in opposition to the promise he had made to Christ.

Verses 58—60:
And after a little while another saw him, and said, Thou art also of them. And Peter said, Man, I am not.

And about the space of one hour after another confidently affirmed, saying, Of a truth this fellow also was with him: for he is a Galilaean.

And Peter said, Man, I know not what thou sayest. And immediately, while he yet spake, the cock crew.

This is very unique. Jesus Christ told him that he would deny him three times before the cock would crow, and just as he denied him the third time, at that instant, the cock crew.

Verse 61:
And the Lord turned, and looked upon Peter. And Peter remembered the word of the Lord, how he had said unto him, Before the cock crow, thou shalt deny me thrice.

The pressure was so heavy and the fear was so intense that Peter did not even realize what he had done until the cock crew. Then the lord looked at him eye to eye. Peter then realized he had denied the Christ whom he loved so dearly, the person he respected more than anyone. He had denied the one he knew in his heart to be the Savior, the only begotten Son of God.

Verse 62:
And Peter went out, and wept bitterly.

Peter's heart was broken. He loved Jesus Christ, and he desired to be a man of God and stand for God with all his being. He wanted to be the kind of man that would risk his life for God's Word; he wanted to be like the great prophets and like Christ. But instead he did the exact opposite; he lied and denied the one whom he had adamantly sworn to go with to the death. Peter failed to be the kind of man he desired to be because of **fear**.

John 20:19a:
Then the same day at evening, being the first day of the week, when the doors were shut where the disciples were assembled for fear of the Jews...

We see Peter (the leader of the disciples) and the rest of them locked behind closed doors, afraid to even go out, fearing those religious Jewish leaders who had crucified the Messiah. There is just nothing more defeating than fear. Fear has ruined more good-hearted Christian men than all other evil combined.

John 20:19b and 20:
...came Jesus and stood in the midst, and saith unto them, Peace be unto you.

And when he had so said, he showed unto them his hands and his side. Then were the disciples glad, when they saw the Lord.

Observe how Christ comforted and encouraged them to overcome their fears. This is always God's will, to help His people live above fear.

In a very short period of time an amazing thing is going to happen to Peter and the apostles. They will be completely set free from fear. By walking forth in the **power** of God, they will be changed from fearful disciples to bold and fearless men of God.

Acts 2:4:
And they [the twelve apostles] were all filled with the Holy Ghost [holy spirit], and began to speak with other tongues, as the Spirit gave them utterance.

These men received the new birth and were filled with holy spirit. The word "filled" means overflowing. The new birth and the overflowing with holy spirit coupled with the Word of God living in their hearts will change Peter and the apostles dynamically.

Verse 14:
But Peter, standing up with the eleven, lifted up his voice, and said unto them, Ye men of Judaea, and all ye that dwell at Jerusalem, be this known unto you, and hearken to my words:

Look at the courage; look at the boldness! Fifty days earlier they were in hiding, afraid to come out of their house. Now, they are confronting the very people who had the Messiah crucified.

Verse 36:
Therefore let all the house of Israel know assuredly, that God hath made that same Jesus, whom ye have crucified, both Lord and Christ.

Peter said, "That same Jesus whom you crucified is both lord and Christ." He looked right in the eyes of the people of whom he was once afraid, and with absolute boldness, absolute courage, and absolute confidence he said, "You crucified the one whom God has made lord and Christ." This is not just an improvement; it is a one hundred percent reversal to total freedom from fear. He was as bold and as fearless as Jesus Christ himself. What delivered him? What changed him?

The only thing that will explosively eliminate the fear in men's and women's lives is the Word living in their hearts in conjunction with the power of the holy spirit overflowing in their lives. When the Word of God lives in a person's heart and he overflows with the power of the holy spirit, at that place, he has perfect love; at that point he cannot be defeated. This is the how, **H-O-W**, of becoming fearless. This is the only thing that will completely cast out your fears. Freedom from fear is extremely available, plus God desires for every child of His to live without fear. It is God's deepest desire for His children to live His Word and operate His power, becoming fully free from fear. It is available. You can do this; and no matter how extreme the fear is, if you **give your whole heart to the power of God and the Word of God**, the fear will dissipate over a short period or, at worst, a moderate period of time.

Acts 4:1—3:
And as they spake unto the people, the priests, and the captain of the temple, and the Sadducees, came upon them,

Being grieved that they taught the people, and preached through Jesus the **resurrection** from the dead.

And they laid hands on them, and put them in hold [in jail] unto the next day: for it was now eventide.

You may be surprised that the spiritual battle has not changed. The very people who counterfeit themselves to be God's people are the ones who fight against the movement of the Word of God. It was the priest, the captain of the temple, and the Sadducees who were trying to hold back the apostles from making the Word live. If you are out holding forth the Word of

God, helping people with that Word, you will be in for a fight at times with people whom you would not expect. Many times they will be religious, claiming to be Christian.

Verse 4:
Howbeit many of them which heard the word believed; and the number of the men was about five thousand.

The religious leaders and their threats could not stop the Word of God from moving; about five thousand people received the new birth.

Verses 5 and 6:
And it came to pass on the morrow, that their rulers, and elders, and scribes,

And Annas the high priest, and Caiaphas, and John, and Alexander, and as many as were of the kindred of the high priest, were gathered together at Jerusalem.

All the highest-ranking religious leaders were going to back these apostles down. They had the Ph.D.s, they had the money, they were in governmental power, and they had the lawyers behind them.

Verse 7:
And when they had set them in the midst, they asked, By what power, or by what name, have ye done this?

Now they are putting the pressure on the apostles.

Verse 8:
Then Peter, filled with the Holy Ghost, said unto them, Ye rulers of the people, and elders of Israel,

The word "filled" means overflowing; "Holy Ghost" is holy spirit. Peter was overflowing with holy spirit.

Verses 9 and 10:
If we this day be examined of the good deed done to the impotent man, by what means he is made whole;

Be it known unto you all, and to all the people of Israel, that by the name of Jesus Christ of Nazareth, whom ye crucified, whom God raised from the dead, even by him doth this man stand here before you whole.

Look at the courage of Peter. All the highly educated, governmentally powerful, big-money people were stacked against him. Yet, he looked them square in the face with absolute boldness and said, "You crucified him (Jesus Christ). And it is by his name that this man is delivered."

Verses 11—13:
This is the stone which was set at nought of you builders, which is become the head of the corner.

Neither is there salvation in any other: for there is none other **name** under heaven given among men, whereby we must be saved.

Now when they saw the boldness of Peter and John, and perceived that they were unlearned and ignorant men, they marvelled; and they took knowledge of them, that they had been with Jesus.

In verse 13 "unlearned and ignorant" means that they did not have their Ph.D.s like the Pharisees, nor were they formally trained in the law and religious tradition, as were the religious hierarchy. Yet they had superior confidence and superior wisdom. They were tapped into God, speaking for God without any fear.

Verse 17:
But that it spread no further among the people,
let us straitly threaten them, that they speak
henceforth to no man in this name.

"Straitly threaten them...." This is the
adversary's primary tool. If he can poison you
with fear, he can defeat you.

Verses 21—24:
So when they had further threatened them,
they let them go, finding nothing how they
might punish them, because of the people: for
all men glorified God for that which was done.

For the man was above forty years old, on
whom this miracle of healing was showed.

And being let go, they went to their own
company, and reported all that the chief priests
and elders had said unto them.

And when they heard that, they lifted up their
voice to God with one accord, and said, Lord,
thou art God, which hast made heaven, and
earth, and the sea, and all that in them is:

Verses 25—29:
Who by the mouth of thy servant David hast said, Why did the heathen rage, and the people imagine vain things?

The kings of the earth stood up, and the rulers were gathered together against the Lord, and against his Christ.

For of a truth against thy holy child Jesus, whom thou hast anointed, both Herod, and Pontius Pilate, with the Gentiles, and the people of Israel, were gathered together,

For to do whatsoever thy hand and thy counsel determined before to be done.

And now, Lord, behold their threatenings: and grant unto thy servants, that with all boldness they may speak thy word,

Speaking the Word is what got them into trouble, put in jail. What did they ask God to give them? Did they ask for an addition to their house, a vacation home, or a shinier car? No. They asked for even more boldness to speak God's Word. They did not want one little dot of fear to creep into their lives.

Verses 30 and 31:
By stretching forth thine hand to heal; and that signs and wonders may be done by the name of thy holy child Jesus.

And when they had prayed, the place was shaken where they were assembled together; and they were all filled with the Holy Ghost, and they spake the word of God with boldness.

If the average church was shaken, you would not see those people again; they would be scared to come back.

The apostles received the answer to their prayer and continued speaking the Word of God with great boldness.

The way to overcome fear is to know the Word of God, most importantly, to do or live the Word of God, and to be dynamically overflowing with the holy spirit—not dripping and dropping, but overflowing. When and where the spirit of God overflows in a person's life and the Word of God is lived, he will have great power; he will have perfect love, which consummates into freedom from fear.

A highly important factor in successful living is **learning to be honest with God,** weeding out your secret fears with God's help. You must learn to operate God's power, which will cleanse and heal your heart, causing you to have the life you have dreamed of, free of fear.

These verses in II Chronicles exemplify the fearless heart of trusting God.

II Chronicles 32:7 and 8:
Be strong and courageous, be not afraid nor dismayed for the king of Assyria, nor for all the multitude that is with him: for there be more with us than with him:

With him is an arm of flesh; but with us is the LORD our God to help us, and to fight our battles. And the people rested themselves upon the words of Hezekiah king of Judah.

The how of overcoming fear is to operate the power of the holy spirit and to live God's Word. The how to stay fearless is to trust God and His Word as Hezekiah did, not relying on your senses information.

CHAPTER 4

The Psychology of Believing

In "The Psychology of Believing," we will deal with three simple words: "mind," "heart," and "believing."

"Mind" is the Greek word *nous*, meaning the organ of mental perception. The second word "heart" is Greek *kardia*. The definitions for "heart" are as follows: (1) your innermost being; (2) the part of your mind that contains what makes you you; (3) the center of your mental perception where your convictions, your innermost feelings, and the very essence of who you are resides, the place where all your decisions are made.

Proverbs 23:7a:
For as he thinketh in his heart, so is he...

Proverbs 27:19:
As in water face answereth to face, so the heart of man to man.

The third word we are studying is "believing," which is the Greek word *pistis*. This word is almost self-explanatory. What one really believes, truly expects, or is genuinely convinced about will come to pass.*

Believe is a verb; it connotes action, mental or physical. In order to have a firm grasp on believing, let's consider some simple illustrations.

If you believed it was going to rain on Tuesday, you would not plan Tuesday for a beach picnic. If you were a football enthusiast and believed you had the potential to be a great football player, you would try out for your high school team. However, if you were a football enthusiast and believed you had little or no potential, you would not try out for the team. If you were a young high school male and you believed that the prettiest girl in your school thought you were the greatest, you would call her up and ask her out. However, if you believed she would not give you the time of day, you would not call her. If you needed a job and saw an ad in the paper for a high-paying job you liked and you believed God would give you this job, you would go apply. But if you believed you had no chance,

---

*There are some variables that we will discuss in the chapter "The Parameters of Believing."

you would not even bother to apply. If a person believes the Bible is the Truth and it has all the answers to life and the problems therein, he will study the Bible. However, if he believes it is full of myths, errors, and out-dated opinions, he will not seek after biblical truth.

What we believe about ourselves is who we are. What we believe about our lives is what we receive in life. You can change what you believe about yourself with the power and Word of God, and you can go where you want to in life by learning to believe the Word of God.

Romans 5:17b:
...they which receive abundance of grace and of the gift of righteousness shall reign in life by one, Jesus Christ.)

Before we continue, it is essential that you realize people are always believing, at all times. It is so easy to do that you are believing whether you want to or not. It is not a question of whether or not someone is believing; it is **whether he is believing rightly or wrongly**. All defeat is due to wrong believing. One of the great purposes of the Word of God is to learn how to believe rightly and maintain that right believing. Wrong believing will always be detrimental to a person's life, but right believing, which is believing according to the accuracy and precision of God's Word, will bring success to you in every phase and facet of life.

Looking at the diagram below, you will see the larger circle which is the *nous,* the organ of mental perception. Inside the mind, *nous*, is the heart. The heart is the innermost part of your being, as Romans 10:10 states, "...for with the heart man believeth."

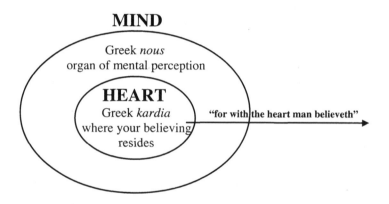

Your mind perceives everything that is introduced to you by your five senses. Everything your ears hear enters your mind, everything your eyes see enters your mind, etc., etc. The thoughts you have in your mind are not what you believe; they are merely thoughts that have been introduced to you. For example, if you watch a boxing match with your best friend, you might look at him and have a thought of bopping him in the head. This is nothing more that a fleeting thought of no consequence. People have millions of these inconsequential thoughts in less than a year.

However, when you have a thought in your mind and you begin to entertain that thought, keep it, and build corresponding thoughts, this thought pattern is beginning to become a part of your life. And the **conviction** with which you carry this thought pattern will determine how quickly it enters your heart. If there is great conviction with the thought pattern, it could proceed from the mind to the heart in a split second. The conviction must be very strong though. Once this enters your heart, it is you; it is your believing, and your life will proceed in the direction of what you have allowed in your heart.

Believing is the greatest principle of life, and, even more crucially, it is the most important principle in the Word of God. Whenever a person takes a promise of God into his mind with great conviction, it will enter his heart, he will believe, and he will receive the benefits and blessings of that promise. By learning these truths and developing trust, believing, in God's Word, you can become more than a conqueror and reign in life by Jesus Christ.

By the power of God and the Word of God, a person can change what he believes in his heart. Sometimes the change is quick, and sometimes the patterns of guilt, fear, and inadequacies are embedded deeply; then it takes more effort and time with God's Word to change his heart. However, anyone can change anything in his life with the power of God if he puts forth the committed effort and stays faithful to it. This is exactly how to achieve the following verse.

Romans 8:37:
Nay, in all these things we are more than conquerors through him that loved us.

Romans 12:2 further explains the process:

And be not conformed to this world: but be ye transformed by the renewing of your mind, that ye may prove what is that good, and acceptable, and perfect, will of God.

"And be not conformed [fashioned] to this world...." How are you fashioned to this world? What you take into your mind through your senses and dwell on fashions you, shapes you to the world with all its misery.

"...But be ye transformed...." The definition of the word "transformed" is to change into another form. You are being exhorted not to be fashioned to the world, continuously changing in a downward, detrimental fashion, but to change who you are in a positive, loving, and godly fashion. The Greek word for "transformed" is *metamorphoo*, from which we get the word "metamorphosis" used of a caterpillar changing into a butterfly. This is representative of the beauty, splendor, and freedom that is ours as we change into living as sons of God.

How do we change our believing to reign in life? "...By the renewing of your mind [*nous*]...." This is the how of Christian success. The Greek word for "renewing" is *anakainosis*, meaning a continuous changing of the thoughts up to the powerful positives of God's Word. Some people change their minds just to be positive. This will work sometimes and fail others. But changing your mind to the positives of God's Word always produces wonderful results.

Simply stated, rather than letting the world fill our minds full of fears, worries, dishonesties, and suspicions, we are to take the wonderful Word of God and continuously bring it to the forefront of our minds throughout our daily lives. This will change us into powerful sons of God, conquering small and difficult situations. This is how you can change to be the person you desire to be. As you begin to put the Word of God in your mind faithfully, that Word will reach your heart. And when it reaches your heart, you will be changed and manifest the great power of God and you will receive answers to prayers.

- You put the Word of God in your mind (*nous*).
- When you are convinced about it, it reaches your heart (*kardia*).
- At the point it reaches your heart, you are believing (*pisteuo*) rightly, believing in God's Word.

This is how simple it is to believe God.

CHAPTER 5

The Parameters of Believing

Positive and negative believing work for the child of God and the unbeliever alike. Believing God's Word works for the child of God. The child of God who **accurately** knows God's Word can believe **much more** because he knows more.[*] Even though believing the Word of God has much greater power and blessings than just positive believing, God has certainly placed parameters, limits, upon what you can do with the great power of believing God.

The first thing you must know in order to operate the great power of believing God's Word is what is available. I have seen knowledge-lacking believers, time and time again, try to believe God to bring to pass things that God's Word declares He will not do. For instance, I knew three young ladies who were trying to believe God to marry the same man. Certainly,

---

[*]People who only know parts of God's Word can be very inaccurate and confused, which causes them to reap very few benefits.

61

you have to be positive, and you can believe God to work with you to help relationships, but each person has freedom of will and God will never overstep it. All three of the ladies married someone else. You can help others, but it is impossible to control others in any way by the power of God. God gave every man freedom of will, and there is no repentance of God's gifts.

Romans 11:29:
For the gifts and calling of God are without repentance.

Since the dawn of time, the true God has never taken over anyone, controlled anyone, or forced anyone to do something. All controlling of people, possession, channeling, and manipulation of others is through the power of the devil via devil spirit possession. From Genesis to Revelation there is never even one account of God controlling an individual. If God controlled people, it would surely make things easy, as well as incomprehensibly boring; for if people were controlled, they would be little more than computers. Whenever you hear someone say, "I don't know what came over me," "I was out of control," "I don't know what possessed me to shoot him," "God made me do it," or, "God took me over," it is always from the wrong god (the devil) and devil spirit possession.

Hosea 4:6:
My people are destroyed for lack of knowledge...

God's people are destroyed for a lack of knowledge. They do not accurately know the promises of God; they do not know how to pray according to God's Word; they do not know how to separate truth from error with God's Word; they do not know how to study and rightly divide the Word of God. This lack of an accurate knowledge and understanding of God's Word has destroyed God's own people. They must learn what is available. If they think it is available for God to control them, these thoughts make them vulnerable to the adversary. If they think they can control others, they will fall flat on their faces. You cannot believe to make the girl of your choice like you or vice versa. You cannot believe to cause another person to do anything you want; it is impossible. You can encourage people, build people's confidence, comfort them, and love them, yet even your own siblings will make their own decisions and choices.

Jeremiah 2:13:
For my people have committed two evils; they have forsaken me the fountain of living waters, and hewed them out cisterns, broken cisterns, that can hold no water.

Some people and even some of God's people pray to Jesus. Yet Jesus Christ always, without any exception taught people to pray to God, and he always, without exception prayed to God. There are literally over a hundred verses in the New Testament either commanding us to pray to God, teaching us to pray to God, or in which prayer is being made to God. There are no verses teaching, commanding, or showing prayer to Jesus. Those who pray to Jesus have hewed out their own cistern, a broken cistern that can hold no water. They have not gone to God's Word which He gave them to live by. It sounds really nice and religious, but it is totally contrary to God's will which is His Word. For, Jesus Christ gave his life to give you full access to God your Father so when you pray to God in the name of Jesus Christ,* you receive answers to prayers.

Ephesians 3:11 and 12:
According to the eternal purpose which he [God] purposed in Christ Jesus our Lord:

In whom [Jesus Christ] we have boldness and **access** with confidence by the faith of him.

---

*Ephesians 5:20: **Giving thanks always for all things unto God and the Father in the name of our Lord Jesus Christ;**
Also see Colossians 3:17.

Ephesians 2:17 and 18:
And came and preached peace to you which
were afar off, and to them that were nigh.

For **through** him [Jesus Christ] we both have
access by one Spirit unto the Father.

Another great practical error is seeking
fellowship and guidance with angels. This occurs
when people have hewed out their own cisterns,
forsaking God and His Word. The only angels
they will receive fellowship and guidance from
are fallen angels (devil spirits). If the Bible, the
Word of God, is true, we are to seek fellowship
with God our Father and the family in which He
has put us.

There is no occurrence in the Bible of men
of God ever **seeking** after angels for guidance.
On **rare** occasions, God sent His angels with
special instructions. The very greatest men in the
Bible received instructions from angels[*] only two
or three times during their lives. Yet, every day
of their lives, they sought direction from God and
He gave it to them. It is available to receive

---

[*]You cannot believe to receive aid or instruction from an angel
because it is not promised in God's Word. When it happens,
which is genuinely rare, it is God's prerogative. It has nothing to
do with man's believing. In His infinite knowledge and wisdom,
God deems it necessary.

direction from God many times in one day. This is called "walking with God," and those who commit themselves to learn and do God's Word will develop this wonderful walk. However, not **ONE** person in the Bible developed a walk with an angel, for it is **not available from the true God**. Regular guidance from angels is a broken cistern people have hewed out themselves, as opposed to studying God's Word. This will reap destruction in their lives over time.

If you want to operate the power of God, receive the great promises of God, and develop the sweet walk with God, you must start by learning what is available.

You cannot bring any evil to pass by believing God, not even revenge on those who have mistreated you.

Luke 9:54 and 55:
And when his disciples James and John saw this, they said, Lord, wilt thou that we command fire to come down from heaven, and consume them, even as Elias did?

But he turned, and rebuked them, and said, Ye know not what manner of spirit ye are of.

Romans 12:19:
Dearly beloved, avenge not yourselves, but rather give place unto wrath: for it is written, Vengeance is mine; I will repay, saith the Lord.

We have already learned **how to receive the promises of God**; that is by believing. You must study God's Word to learn what is available and what is not available from God.

CHAPTER 6

The Three Part Man

It is a common teaching throughout Christian religious organizations that man is a two part man: body and soul. But the Bible is very lucid describing man as a three-part man: body, soul, and spirit. The simple, obvious biblical truth of man being three parts (body, soul, and spirit) will clarify hundreds of discrepancies and misconceptions. Understanding the three-part man is an absolute necessity for the biblical student to be able to separate truth from error. It brings us back to the exact and precise Word of God. Spirit, **the most important part of man**, is the missing or muddled part.

The great truth of the three-part man is stated in I Thessalonians 5:23.

I Thessalonians 5:23:
And the very God of peace sanctify you
wholly; and I pray God your whole **spirit and
soul and body** be preserved blameless unto
the coming of our Lord Jesus Christ.

"Your whole spirit and soul and body...."
Do these three words "spirit," "soul," and "body"
have the same meaning? Of course not. They are
evidently different words. Yet, people have taken
the liberty to use them interchangeably, as though
they have the same meaning. They are in no way
synonymous, and the Greek words from which
they are translated are in no way related to each
other. They have been translated correctly, and
they have three distinctly different meanings.

In elucidating the truth of man having three
parts, we need to study Isaiah 43:7:

Even every one that is called by my name: for
I have **created** him for my glory, I have
formed him; yea, I have **made** him.

Are the three words "created," "formed,"
and "made" the same in meaning? Of course not.
They are three distinct words with three different
meanings, and God placed them there precisely as
they should be to explain the truth of what
man is.

Let's allow the Word of God to show us what Isaiah 43:7 is declaring when it says, "I [God] have formed him [man]."

Genesis 2:7:
And the LORD God formed man of the dust of the ground, and breathed into his nostrils the breath of life; and man became a living soul.

Yatsar is the Hebrew word for "formed." Its meaning is "to form or fashion as a potter would form a pot out of clay (to use something already in existence, like clay for a pot)." God formed man of the dust of the ground, and we are called "earthen vessels." Man's body is composed of elements from the earth. The meaning of the word "Adam" is "red earth." Our bodies are earthen or clay vessels, this being the least important part of man.

Ecclesiastes 3:20:
All go unto one place; all are of the dust, and all turn to dust again.

Genesis 3:19:
In the sweat of thy face shalt thou eat bread, till thou return unto the ground; for out of it wast thou taken: **for dust thou art, and unto dust shalt thou return**.

It is clear that man's body was formed of the dust of the ground. Hebrews says, "...it is appointed unto men once to die," and we just read that all men will return to dust. Therefore, all men's bodies will be dust again.

The following step in this study is to determine what a man's soul is. The soul is superior to the body of man in that it is the life of man. It is that which makes him a living being. We will see clearly that it is not what people have commonly taught. For, the animal kingdom, or animals, have soul life, just as man has soul life. The soul makes the formed body of man alive.

Genesis 2:7b:
...and breathed into his nostrils the breath of life; and man became a living soul [*nephesh*].

There is a great truth here; when a newborn baby or a newborn animal breathes in for the first time, something happens, untraceable to the scientific man, that causes the person or animal to be a living soul. This is how God has ordered and set up soul life. The same holds true for the last breath. When the person or animal breathes for the last time, the life, the soul, has departed out of him.

The erroneous teaching that one's soul lives forever or that it is the part of the Christian that gives him eternal life is nothing more than conjecture and has no biblical accuracy. According to the Word of God, it is the spirit that is eternal. It is the spirit that, when given to a person, causes him to be a true Christian. It is the spirit that is the highest life form ever created by God.

Continuing to study the word "soul," we will see that animals are living souls, just as men are.

Genesis 1:30:
And to every beast of the earth, and to every fowl of the air, and to every thing that creepeth upon the earth, wherein there is life...

The word "life" is *nephesh*, the same word used for man's soul. All animals have soul life, as well as man, and this is not the part of life that makes man truly superior to the animals.

Genesis 1:20:
And God said, Let the waters bring forth abundantly the moving creature that hath life, and fowl that may fly above the earth in the open firmament of heaven.

In Genesis 1:20, the words "that hath" are added. The word "creature" is *nephesh*, which means "soul," and the word "life" is *chai*. Therefore, "creature that hath life" should be translated "living soul." These are the exact same two words used for man being a living soul.

Genesis 1:20 should read:

And God said, Let the waters bring forth abundantly the moving living soul...

Verse 21:
And God created great whales, and every living creature [*nephesh chai*, living soul]...

Verse 24:
And God said, Let the earth bring forth the living creature after his kind, cattle, and creeping thing, and beast of the earth after his kind: and it was so.

"Living creature" is *nephesh chai*, living soul. There are many other places in the Bible where these words are used of man and of animals.

The scriptures are exacting; every man has soul life, and that soul life is not eternal and has nothing to do with being a Christian. Observe carefully Acts 3:23:

> And it shall come to pass, that every soul, which will not hear that prophet, shall be destroyed from among the people.

It states that every soul which does not hear that prophet shall be destroyed. The prophet spoken of in this verse is Jesus Christ the Son of God. Those who do not believe that Jesus Christ is the Son of God, who reject him, shall be destroyed. The soul life cannot be eternal; it has no relationship to being a Christian and is common to every man and animal.[*]

It is interesting to note that all living souls, man and animals, have blood, and Leviticus 17:11 says, "...the life of the flesh is in the blood." The word "life" again is *nephesh*, soul.

---

[*]**Romans 2:9: Tribulation and anguish, upon every soul of man that doeth evil, of the Jew first, and also of the Gentile;**
Acts 27:37: And we were in all in the ship two hundred threescore and sixteen souls.
I Peter 3:20: Which sometime were disobedient, when once the longsuffering of God waited in the days of Noah, while the ark was a preparing, wherein few, that is, eight souls were saved by water.

It is also of significance to observe that when you breathe in, the oxygen does not directly reach your brain, but progresses through your blood to reach all parts of your body.

Acts 17:26:
And hath made of one blood all nations of men for to dwell on all the face of the earth, and hath determined the times before appointed, and the bounds of their habitation;

All men have the same blood in their veins. All of our soul life is derived from that one man Adam. Recently, some genetic scientists have proven that all men and all races came from one man. Of course, we who believe God's Word already knew this. The simple reason for different races of men is nothing more than the genetic laws and variations God set in Adam when he made him and over the centuries men's bodies, hair, skin-coloring, etc. adapt to the environment in which they live, making them more distinctly different.

We must remember and adhere to the biblical truth that the soul life of man departs with his last breath when he dies. The biblical timing of life is the first breath, and the biblical timing of death is the last breath; thus man's body returns to dust.

Now we will delve into the greatest part of man, the spirit, that which makes man exceedingly superior to the animals, that which determines whether he is a child of God (Christian) who lives forever or just an ordinary man of body and soul who dies and remains dead forever.

First, we must understand the word "create."

Genesis 1:1:
In the beginning God created the heaven and the earth.

This word "create" is misused a lot in our society. People say that someone is creative—impossible from a biblical standpoint. God is the Creator and the only One who has the ability to create. There is none other than God who has the power and ability to create. People can take things that God has created and make something from them. They may make something that is unique, but they are not creative and they cannot create. The word "create" used in this way is a misnomer prompted usually by egotism. The word "create," *bara* in Hebrew, means to cause something to exist that has not previously existed (in any shape, form, or fashion). There is only one Creator, and that is God.

Genesis 1:3:
And God said, Let there be light: and there was light.

Note in Genesis 1:3 God did not create light. He merely spoke it into being from that which He had created in Genesis 1:1.

Verse 6 and 11:
And God said, Let there be a firmament in the midst of the waters...

And God said, Let the earth bring forth grass, the herb yielding seed, and the fruit tree yielding fruit after his kind, whose seed is in itself, upon the earth: and it was so.

This is the pattern. Once God creates something, He no longer needs to create anymore. He only changes what He has created to make new things. Note carefully verse 21:

And God created great whales, and every living creature that moveth, which the waters brought forth abundantly, after their kind, and every winged fowl after his kind: and God saw that it was good.

Here is the word "created." The elements of which their bodies were made had already been created. God did not need to create their bodies. Both water and earth were already there to make their bodies so what did God create here? "Living creature" again is *nephesh chai*, soul life. This is what God had not yet created. In verse 21 God created soul life. Later, when He formed, made, and created man, He did not create soul life; it was already in existence. Yet, He certainly created something magnificent. Look at Genesis 1:27:

> So God created man in his own image, in the image of God created he him; male and female created he them.

Three times the word "create" is used in this verse. No other time in the Bible is such emphasis put upon the greatness of what God created. This was God's greatest creation, God's masterpiece, the culmination of what He desired and wanted. Verse 27 states twice that He created man in His image, establishing it so it cannot be denied.

What does "God created man in His own image" mean? It cannot be referring to their bodies because he created male and female in His own image and a male's and a female's bodies are uniquely different. Certainly soul life, which every animal has, is not the image of God. The answer lies in John 4.24:

God is a Spirit...

By creating man in His image, God was fulfilling His highest desire: to have dearly beloved friends to converse and communicate with, to walk hand in hand and heart in heart with as beloved companions. The spirit in man was that which enabled man and God to be at one, to have sweet fellowship. It was man's primary source of learning and enjoyment. The spirit gave man true and perpetual life.

Genesis 1:26:
And God said, Let us make man in our image, after our likeness: and let them have dominion over the fish of the sea, and over the fowl of the air, and over the cattle, and over all the earth, and over every creeping thing that creepeth upon the earth.

It was the spirit of God created in man that gave him power and dominion over all the earth.

I Thessalonians 5:23: ...your whole spirit
and soul and body...

Isaiah 43:7: ... I have created him
for my glory, I have formed him;
yea, I have made him.

BODY SOUL SPIRIT

formed	*made*	*created*
dust of the earth	previously created	likeness or image of God
The body is composed of the elements.	breath life	life eternal
returns to dust	common to man and animals	our full connection to God

CHAPTER 7

The Fall of Adam (Mankind)

In the first few chapters of Genesis, many of life's basic truths are set forth. We are about to examine a few of them.

Genesis 1:1 and 2:
In the beginning God created the heaven and the earth.

And the earth was without form, and void; and darkness was upon the face of the deep. And the Spirit of God moved upon the face of the waters.

"And the earth was without form, and void" should read: "And the earth **became** without form and void." This Hebrew word *hayah* is translated "became" throughout Genesis and should be. The word "became" is very important because Isaiah 45:18 states that God did not originally create the earth without form and void.

Isaiah 45:18:
For thus saith the LORD that created the heavens; God himself that **formed the earth** and made it; he hath established it, he created it **not in vain**, he formed it to be inhabited...

In Genesis 1:2 the two words "without form" are one word in Hebrew, *tohuw*. It means desolate, a wasteland, useless, and empty. In Isaiah 45:18 the word "vain" is the word *tohuw* again, but in Isaiah it states that God created the earth not *tohuw*, destroyed and wasted. Isaiah states that God Himself formed the earth and He made it perfectly to provide for its inhabitants. Genesis 1:2 declares that it became a desolate wasteland.

In Genesis 1:1 when God created the heaven and the earth, He created it perfectly, as stated in Isaiah. But between Genesis 1:1 and 1:2, a great catastrophe took place. There was war in heaven, and Lucifer, one of the three archangels, the most exalted, rebelled or mutinied against God. And one third of all the angels, those under Lucifer's command, were cast out of heaven. Lucifer with one third of the angels now constitute all the devil spirits in the evil spirit realm. After Lucifer's fall, he is now called the devil, and the fallen angels under his command are called "devil spirits."[*] This large body of non-visible evil-doers are the **power and perpetrators behind all wickedness that occurs in the world**.

The earth became without form and void. The war in heaven was so great that the earth was desolate and all living beings of that time were destroyed. God's original creation of the earth becoming without form and void will answer hundreds of scientific questions and problems. The prehistoric man that scientists find is not the same man of today. The skeletal system may be similar, but according to God's Word, soul life was not created until later in Genesis 1:21. Therefore, the prehistoric man that had similarities in his skeletal system to current man is **not even the same life form** as current man.

If the scientists would come back to God's Word and start their work from a premise of Truth rather that errant suppositions, they would save millions upon millions of dollars and millions upon millions of man hours, all wasted because of erroneous theories contrived by man's ego rather than the Truth of God's Word.

---

[*]**Ezekial 28:15: Thou wast perfect in thy ways from the day that thou wast created, till iniquity was found in thee.**
Revelation 12:4: And his tail drew the third part of the stars of heaven, and did cast them to the earth: and the dragon stood before the woman which was ready to be delivered, for to devour her child as soon as it was born.

The Fall of Adam (Mankind)

For thousands of years, all of the great scientific minds of the world had believed and propounded that the world was flat, but an avid Bible student and cartographer named Christopher Columbus defied their erroneous theory and believed what was written in the scroll of Isaiah approximately 600 years before Christ, that the world was round or a circle.

The theory of evolution of our time is just as the theory of the world being flat. In some of our schools they teach it as if it has been proven, but on the contrary, it is still a theory, and millions of dollars and man hours have been squandered trying to prove the theory of evolution, yet always failing. When I was a young boy, they combed Africa searching for the missing link and the rumored sightings of peculiar white apes, not to mention the folly of the Abominable Snowman. And even at this time, millions of dollars are being spent to find another creature that does not exist—Bigfoot. Almost innumerable studies, writings, and laboratory testings have been done to find the missing link that would prove the theory of evolution. You would think forty years of abject failure might cast a little doubt on their theory, but not so. Some of the teachers even avoid admitting to their students that it is a theory.

Genesis 1:28:
And God blessed them, and God said unto them, Be fruitful, and multiply, and replenish the earth, and subdue it: and have dominion over the fish of the sea, and over the fowl of the air, and over every living thing that moveth upon the earth.

God said, "Replenish the earth." Therefore, the previous earth had to have been inhabited. Scientists try to include prehistoric man in the same genus with man, but what they call prehistoric man was not the same type of life we currently have. Man is a genus, and he is the only species in his genus. We will see this in Genesis 1:21:

And God created great whales, and every living creature that moveth, which the waters brought forth abundantly, after their kind, and every winged fowl after his kind: and God saw that it was good.

The word "kind" in verse 21 is the Old Testament word for "genus."[*] Since the dawn of

---

[*] **We get our word "genus" from the Greek word *genos*, but scientists have corrupted its original meaning from the Word. Biblical usage of *genos* in the Old Testament would correspond closer to "families" in today's scientific classification. The Bible clearly depicted the word long before the scientists used it and then abused it.**

time, no one has ever crossed a genus. For instance, you can cross a German Shepherd with a Cocker Spaniel because they are in the same genus; they are both dogs. You will end up with a "cocky German." However, you cannot cross a dog and a cat or a horse and a cow because each is a genus. God said, "everything...after his kind," and it cannot be broken. There is interbreeding and evolution among species of the same genus, but God said that genus always remains the same and that settles it.

For further corroboration, look at Genesis 1:11:

And God said, Let the earth bring forth grass, the herb yielding seed, and the fruit tree yielding fruit after his kind, whose seed is in itself, upon the earth: and it was so.

"Kind" again is the word "genus." This truth stands even in the plant kingdom.

"Whose seed is in itself" refers to the continuance of life. The life is in the seed. The soul life of man is in the seed, and the seed is in the male sperm. This becomes significant when you study the birth of Jesus Christ, for God placed seed in Mary's egg. God has put life in these seeds and they perpetuate much of the life on earth. A tiny seed becomes a great tree and that great tree produces many seeds, replenishing the earth. The same holds true for man.

The focal point and the center of God's creation was the earth. On the earth was where He would place His all-important and highly prized creation: the three part man. Certainly it was not the size of the earth that constituted its greatness. Its greatness was because of the man who God created in His own image. This spirit-filled man was to be God's closest companion, His dearest friend, His treasured child.

Genesis 1:26:
And God said, Let us make man in our image, after our likeness: and let them have dominion over the fish of the sea, and over the fowl of the air, and over the cattle, and over all the earth, and over every creeping thing that creepeth upon the earth.

Again, we see man being in the image of God doubled. Then it says, "Let them have dominion." The word "dominion" means to rule over, to have power and authority over. The verse also states, "...over all the earth." So God's jewel of creation, the earth, was ruled over by His treasured child and beloved friend Adam.

The Fall of Adam (Mankind)

God laid down one commandment to Adam. Other than that, Adam was free to do as he pleased. But he had one commandment that demanded absolute compliance.

Genesis 2:16 and 17:
And the LORD God commanded the man, saying, Of every tree of the garden thou mayest freely eat:

But of the tree of the knowledge of good and evil, thou shalt not eat of it: for in the day that thou eatest thereof thou shalt surely die.

"But of the tree of knowledge of good and evil, **thou shalt not eat of it**...." Make a mental marker of this. "For **in the day** that thou eatest thereof **thou shalt surely die**." This is crystal clear: the day you eat you shall **surely** die. This commandment is not bemusing, but as simple as black and white.

At this point, Adam had perfect harmony with God; he walked with God and talked with God not a little. The part of Adam that gave him the power to have dominion over the earth and to have this constant communication and sweetness with God was spirit. Spirit is the source of true life, perfect life, eternal life. Spirit cannot die, nor can it wear or wax old; it is constant.

The Fall of Adam (Mankind)

In Genesis chapter 3 Adam's cataclysmic disaster unfolds.

Genesis 3:1:
Now the serpent was more subtle than any beast of the field which the LORD God had made. And he said unto the woman, Yea, hath God said, Ye shall not eat of every tree of the garden?

Notice it states that the serpent was more subtle than anything God had made. The word "subtle" means wise, but it is used in a sly, crafty sense here. The Hebrew word for "serpent" also puts emphasis on his seductive charm. The serpent questioned God's Word. He has not changed; this is still his first step in defeating believers, to make them doubt the veracity of God's Word. The integrity of the Truth of God's Word is always at stake.

The proper response would have been, "Get out of here, Satan," and then to quote the Word accurately. However, Eve **considered** the words of the adversary. Whenever you use your **reason** to deal with the onslaughts of the adversary, you will be defeated. No person using his intellect can stand up to the craftiness of the adversary. It is the power and truth from God's Word that cause people to prevail over the adversary.

The devil is far too wise to come at you directly and openly. He slowly, slyly seduces you to doubt God's Word. Once you consider his words and use your logic, you are heading straight down. But when you adamantly stand on the truth that you believe, he will flee from you.[*]

Verse 2:
And the woman said unto the serpent, We may eat of the fruit of the trees of the garden:

In verse 2 not only is Eve considering, but she is conversing with the devil. Then she omits the word "freely" from God's commandment. This a fatal mistake. **When a word is omitted from the Truth, all you have is error**; it is no longer God's words; it is no longer perfect and no longer the Truth.

If your boss told you to buy fifty loaves of bread at the market for the company picnic and you returned with five loaves and said, "Here's some bread for the picnic," he would be disturbed with you and probably disappointed. The so-called Christian religious world has respected God's Word so little that even men's words receive more respect than God's Word.

---

[*]**James 4:7: Submit yourselves therefore to God. Resist the devil, and he will flee from you.**

To respect men's words above God's Word is a great insult to the Heavenly Father.

Verse 3:
But of the fruit of the tree which is in the midst of the garden, God hath said, Ye shall not eat of it, neither shall ye touch it, lest ye die.

Now Eve added, "...neither shall ye touch it."

Revelation 22:18 and 19:
For I testify unto every man that heareth the words of the prophecy of this book, If any man shall add unto these things, God shall add unto him the plagues that are written in this book:

And if any man shall take away from the words of the book of this prophecy, God shall take away his part out of the book of life, and out of the holy city, and from the things which are written in this book.

These two verses speak clearly as to the supreme importance of keeping God's Word pure.

Observe that Eve stated, "...lest ye die," but God had said, "In the day thou eatest thereof thou shalt surely die." Eve changed God's Word from the absolute: "thou shalt surely die" to the possibility: "lest, maybe ye die." She no longer believed the Word; she was questioning the Word of Truth herself.

Now we will see where the serpent originally planned to take Eve before he conversed with her.

Verse 4:
And the serpent said unto the woman, Ye shall not surely die:

God said, "**Thou shalt surely die**." The serpent says, "**Ye shall not surely die**." The serpent's antithetical statement displays him as he truly is—in total opposition to God and His Truth. This lie that the adversary tricked Eve into believing has been propounded by the adversary throughout much of religious Christianity. You could call this the birth of spiritualism:* "Thou shalt not surely die." When someone dies, the minister proclaims he has moved on to a new and better place or his soul is now up in heaven and he is so much better off. If it is so great and so much better to be dead, then logically all of us should desire death. If you go to heaven directly upon dying, then all Christians should commit suicide. You are not really dead is what they teach. The spiritualists teach it, and even the Christian churches teach it, too. This is contrary and in opposition to God's Word from Genesis to Revelation. The Bible clearly and repeatedly states the dead are dead until the return of Christ in the future. By teaching contrary to numerous scriptures, they make the Bible a laughing-stock, mocking Christ's return** and making his return pointless.

---

*Spiritualism here refers to a type of religion which includes seances and other ways to bring people back from the dead. Actually, they conjure up a familiar devil spirit to pose as the dead person. The familiar spirit makes itself familiar with details of people's lives, using the details to convince people it is their lost loved one.

Leviticus 19:31: Regard not them that have familiar spirits, neither seek after wizards, to be defiled by them: I am the LORD your God.

** I Thessalonians 4:16 and 17: For the Lord himself shall descend from heaven with a shout, with the voice of the archangel, and with the trump of God: and the dead in Christ shall rise first:

Then we which are alive and remain shall be caught up together with them in the clouds, to meet the Lord in the air: and so shall we ever be with the Lord.

The following are just a few of very many scriptures that precisely state the dead are dead.

Psalms 6:5:
For in death there is no remembrance of thee: in the grave who shall give thee thanks?

Psalms 146:4:
His breath goeth forth, he returneth to his earth; in that very day his thoughts perish.

Ecclesiastes 9:5 and 6:
For the living know that they shall die: but the dead know not any thing, neither have they any more a reward; for the memory of them is forgotten.

Also their love, and their hatred, and their envy, is now perished; neither have they any more a portion for ever in any thing that is done under the sun.

The Word of God is very precise; those who believe in Jesus as the Christ and confess him as lord will be born again of God's spirit and will be gathered together unto God by the return of Jesus Christ, living forever. On the other hand, those who refuse Christ will be dead forever.

The manner in which the adversary tricked Eve is the same method he uses to deceive people today:

- First, he questioned God's Word.
- Then, he seduced her into considering the question and using her reasoning.
- Next, Eve committed a fatal mistake; she omitted a word from God's Truth.
- Then, she added to God's Word.
- And finally, she changed God's true Word,
- resulting in believing the devil's lie and receiving the terrible consequences.

This is why the people of God today have failed to operate the great power of God as declared in the Gospels and Acts. They have reasoned with their intellects, questioning the Word of God to the point they have changed it. Consequently, they no longer have the Truth.

If Microsoft handled their software programs with the lack of accuracy and detail with which Christians handle the Word of God, they would be bankrupt overnight. And many people who desire to be Christian or are Christian are bankrupt in their hearts. For, not only do they teach the devil's lie "thou shalt not surely die," but they take it a step further and teach the second great lie, that the all-loving, compassionate God, the Father of the lord Jesus Christ, kills little children. Or a small child is told God took his mother from him when the Word of God vehemently proclaims that all life comes from God and all death comes from the devil.[*]

> Hosea 4:6:
>
> **My people are destroyed for lack of knowledge**: because thou hast rejected knowledge, I will also reject thee, that thou shalt be no priest to me: seeing thou hast forgotten the law of thy God, I will also forget thy children.

Hosea 4:6 says that God's people are destroyed for a lack of knowledge. Many people who desire God do not know God's Word accurately and fully to become born again. Many people who are born again do not know their legal sonship rights, how to operate the power of God, nor how to receive answers to prayer. They cannot make the Word flow together with accuracy and detail, which causes them to believe very little of God's Word. Therefore, they are

---

[*]**I Corinthians 15:26: The last enemy that shall be destroyed is death.**
Hebrews 2:14b: ...he also himself likewise took part of the same; that through death he might destroy him that had the power of death, that is, the devil;
John 10:10: The thief cometh not, but for to steal, and to kill, and to destroy: I am come that they might have life, and that they might have it more abundantly.

destroyed for lack of knowledge by the adversary. The devil is always out to destroy the Word of God, for the Word of God teaches a non-Christian how to become a Christian and teaches the Christian how to be more than a conqueror.

Romans 8:37:
Nay, in all these things we are more than conquerors through him that loved us.

How can the Christian believe to be more than a conqueror if he does not know this verse from Romans?

Genesis 3:4 and 5:
And the serpent said unto the woman, Ye shall not surely die:

For God doth know that in the day ye eat thereof, then your eyes shall be opened, and ye shall be as gods, knowing good and evil.

In verse 5 the devil said, "...ye shall be as gods, knowing good and evil." This is exactly where most people are today; they are their own god; they set their own standards for good and evil, no matter how degraded or perverted. Their own intellect and reasoning takes the place of God and His magnificent Word.

Verse 6:
And when the woman saw that the tree was good for food, and that it was pleasant to the eyes, and a tree to be desired to make one wise, she took of the fruit thereof, and did eat, and gave also unto her husband with her; and he did eat.

The woman saw that the tree was good for food, pleasant to the eyes, to be desired. This shows that she went by her five senses and reasoning. The woman then disobeyed, and Adam followed right behind her.

If you study the Word further, Adam and Eve lived on after this. However, God said, "The day thou eatest thereof thou shalt surely die." Then what happened? Adam did die. Adam and Eve **disobeyed God's commandment,** and when they did, they lost the source of all life; the spirit in them went back to God. The spirit is true life; the spirit is pure life; the spirit is eternal life. After this, Adam was only a little more than the animals because he was smarter. His absolute control over the earth was lost. According to God's Word, to lose the spirit is **true** death. The breath life, soul life, of man is minuscule compared to spirit life. When Adam committed this flagrant, foolish act of **disobedience**, he lost his relationship with God. No longer could he receive perfect wisdom to be ruler of the earth. He committed treason against God, and turned over his authority as ruler of the earth to God's enemy, the devil. This disobedience was of such a magnitude that it corrupted Adam's blood and soul life, staining it with sin. All his progeny, mankind, would receive this sin-stained seed and blood from Adam, causing a multiplicity of genetic weaknesses, sickness, sufferings, etc.

Examine carefully other consequences of Adam's disobedience in Luke 4:5 and 6:

And the devil, taking him up into an high mountain, showed unto him all the kingdoms of the world in a moment of time.

And the devil said unto him, All this power will I give thee, and the glory of them: for that is delivered unto me; and to whomsoever I will I give it.

The devil said, "All this power will I give thee." This was once Adam's power. Then he said, "...for that is delivered unto me."

Adam delivered his dominion and authority over the world to the devil. The devil offered this power to Jesus Christ. Just as Adam had the right to give it away, so does the devil. The original sin, which caused imperfection or sin to be in the soul life, the seed, of Adam passed on to all mankind, was high treason against God. Adam turned God's creation, including His cherished companions mankind, over to the devil, God's arch enemy. **The devil being the god of this world and sin being stained in man's blood are the reasons for all sufferings and misery in the world**.

> II Corinthians 4:4:
> In whom **the god of this world** hath blinded the minds of them which believe not, lest the light of the glorious gospel of Christ, who is the image of God, should shine unto them.

The adversary blinds the minds of people the same way he blinded Adam and Eve; their intellect is their god, and they are too egotistically smart to humble themselves to God's Word. The god of this world is the devil. Where do you think hurricanes come from? Floods, famines, wars? Why are some men more vicious than the most vicious animal? Adam has given mankind over from a life of perfect bliss to a life of extreme hardship, from a spirit-filled life of love and power **to have only a corrupted soul**. The devil is the god of this world, and all the humanitarians and politicians are not going to make the world better. The true and greatest help that can be given to people is when knowledgeable Christians teach them the new birth and the power of the holy spirit.

Once you are cognizant of the spiritual realm and the two great spiritual powers, thousands of questions that philosophers and scientists struggle with can be easily answered. All that displays power contrary to God's Word comes from the evil spirit realm. The adversary blinds the minds and hearts of people, preventing them from believing in Christ because God has given Christians power above and over all evil power. The Christian must learn accurately to operate his great power, then he can conquer all evil that besets him.

There are grave consequences when a man rejects Jesus as the Christ.

Psalms 49:11:
Their inward thought is, that their houses shall continue for ever, and their dwelling places to all generations; they call their lands after their own names.

Verses 14 and 19:
Like sheep they are laid in the grave; **death shall feed on them**; and the upright shall have dominion over them in the morning; and their beauty shall consume in the grave from their dwelling.

He shall go to the generation of his fathers; **they shall never** see light.

For those who do not want to believe in Jesus as the Christ, their Savior, Thessalonians states that they "shall be punished with everlasting destruction from the presence of the Lord." Notice here in Psalms it says, "...death shall feed on them," and, "...they shall never see light." They shall be **forever** dead. But for those who desire to know God and be His children, they can become born again of God's spirit, receiving power to live victoriously in this life and the guarantee of a perfect, love-filled life forever, to be God's eternal companions in perfection. In the next chapter we will learn exactly **HOW** to become God's son, filled with His spirit, having the guarantee of perfect and eternal life.

CHAPTER 8

The Belief

HOW does the man of body and soul become a Christian, a three-part man of body, soul, and **spirit**, God's child, His son**? This is the most important question in life**. What if I am not interested in being born again of God's spirit? Then read no further. But if you would like to give God's love a try, if you would like to live forever in perfection, if you would like to avoid death eternal, then continue to read; for, the answers you need will be given in the coming scriptural study.

Our God is so loving and so gracious. He has made it extremely easy to become His child, born again of His spirit. All those who truly desire to be God's sons, born again, can be. There is zero degree of difficulty.

- If you are desiring and meek,
- then you learn how to receive the new birth,
- then you make the decision to do what you have learned,
- you will be made whole, body soul and spirit...

...a three-part being, filled with the spirit of God, born again of spirit, destined for eternal perfection. This is God's grace, His loving kindness; it cannot be achieved by works. The new birth is appropriated by simple believing.

Romans 5:12:
Wherefore, as by one man sin entered into the world, and death by sin; and so death passed upon all men, for that all have sinned:

The one man who sinned is Adam, and he brought sin and death upon all his progeny, mankind.

Verse 15:
But not as the offence, so also is the **free gift**. For if through the offence of one many be dead, much more the grace of God, and the gift by grace, which is by one man, Jesus Christ, hath abounded unto many.

In verse 15 notice the words "free gift." Being born of God's spirit is so magnificent and great that the only way a person can obtain it is by a free gift. It is the gift of a loving God for those in need.

It says, "...through the offence of one many be dead." "One" is Adam. He brought death upon all of mankind. The two words "much more" are very powerful words in Greek. They should be translated "exceedingly exceedingly more." Notice that by one man, Jesus Christ, this gift has abounded to many. One man caused you to be only body and soul, and one man gave his life so you could have the free gift of a sonship spirit.

Romans 5:19:
For as by one man's [Adam's] disobedience many were made sinners, so by the obedience of one [Jesus Christ] shall many be made righteous.

John 14:6:
Jesus saith unto him, I am the way, the truth, and the life: no man cometh unto the Father, but by me.

This verse is a very bold statement. I have studied many of the major religions which contain great names such as Buddha, Confucius, Mohammed, etc., etc. None of these dare make such a bold claim. Nor did any of them claim to be the Christ. The name Jesus was a very common name in biblical times and is still very common in Hispanic countries. It means "savior." But there is only one Jesus the Christ. He is the way, the truth, and the life. And there is no other way to God but by Jesus Christ. If you desire eternal life, to be God's child, you must receive it through belief in Jesus Christ.

John 3:16:
For God so loved the world, that he gave his only begotten Son, that whosoever believeth in him should not perish, but have everlasting life.

God so loved that He gave His only begotten Son. Jesus Christ paid the price, purchased you back from the god of this world to place you in the hands of the God of love. He gave his life for a purpose. That purpose was to pay in full the price of Adam's treason and to buy back mankind to God. He made it available for all who desire to belong to God again and be free from Satan and his influences.

Then it states "whosoever." It means exactly what it says—whosoever. There is no human being who has done anything bad enough to be beneath God's love. And there is nothing anyone can do to be good enough to deserve God's love, His gift of sonship. It can only be by grace.[*]

Last, the verse says, "...everlasting life," not the kind of life you are used to, but a perfect life with a perfect body and a perfect mind. This perfection is in you once you are born again and will come into the fullness when Christ comes back. You receive the perfect spirit now when you become born again, then at Christ's return, your mind and body will be perfected also.

Romans 5:17 and 18:
For if by one man's offence death reigned by one; much more they which receive abundance of grace and of the gift of righteousness shall reign in life by one, Jesus Christ.)

Therefore as by the offence of one judgment came upon all men to condemnation; even so by the righteousness of one the free gift came upon all men unto justification of life.

---

[*]**Ephesians 2:8: For by grace are ye saved through faith; and that not of yourselves: it is the gift of God:**

109

The words "judgment came" are not in any Greek texts; they are added. However, the Greek word for "condemnation" means judgment. Here is a corrected translation of verse 18:

So then as through one transgression there resulted judgment to all men, even so through one act of righteousness there resulted justification of life to all men.[*]

He who believes on Jesus Christ can never again be judged because God makes him righteous the instant he believes. However, he who does not believe on the name of the only begotten Son of God has judged himself unworthy of eternal life.

John 3:36:
He that believeth on the Son hath everlasting life: and he that believeth not the Son shall not see life; but the wrath of God abideth on him.

It is hard to understand why someone would reject the Christ, the Son of God. Yet people certainly do. By believing that Jesus Christ is the Son of God, you can have a power-filled, **more-than-a-conqueror life now**, and perfect,

---

[*] Many times you have to invert words from the Greek texts in order to translate them into an English sentence.

110

everlasting life later. **What have you got to lose?** You have everything to gain by believing, and you have absolutely nothing to lose by believing. Actually, you have everything to lose by rejecting that Jesus is the Christ, the only begotten Son. Why would anyone choose to live this life without God and His loving help and, even more foolishly, reject everlasting life? It has to be because Satan blinds people's hearts and minds.

I Corinthians 2:14:
But the natural man receiveth not the things of the Spirit of God: for they are foolishness unto him: neither can he know them, because they are spiritually discerned.

Until a man is born again of God's spirit, it is very difficult for him to understand the Word. The man of body and soul lacks the capacity to understand God's Word because God's Word is spiritual Truth that can only be understood by a person who is born again of God's spirit. In John 3:3, Jesus declared:

...Except a man be born again, he cannot see the kingdom of God.

Verse 5:

...Except a man be born of water and of the Spirit, he cannot enter into the kingdom of God.

The fleshly first birth is born of water. When the embryonic sac breaks, water comes out of the womb.

Verse 6:

That which is born of the flesh is flesh; and **that which is born of the Spirit is spirit.**

We are literally to be born again of God's spirit to become whole, having all three parts. The phrase "born again" has become a meaningless cliché touted about with little understanding. You will rarely hear "born again of spirit" or "born again of the spirit of God."

I John 3:9:

Whosoever is born of God doth not commit sin; for his seed remaineth in him: and he cannot sin, because he is born of God.

"Whosoever is born of God...." You can be God's child, His son, born again of God's seed.

"Doth not commit sin; for his seed
remaineth in him...." The part of man that does
not commit sin is the spirit. The spirit is perfect;
it is pure life. It cannot and does not sin. Those
who choose to be born again are the very seed of
God. The last part of the verse states, "...he is
born of God." Wouldn't you like to be born
again of God's seed, to have the very spirit of
God in you, to be God's child, to have the future
promise of a perfect mind and body that last
forever?

I Peter 1:23:
Being born again, not of corruptible seed, but
of incorruptible, by the word of God, which
liveth and abideth for ever.

"Being born again of incorruptible seed...."
When you are born of seed, you cannot lose it.
And the spiritual seed of God cannot sin. It is
even more permanent than your first birth.
Certain religious circles commonly teach that you
can be born again one minute (of course, they
leave out seed and spirit) but when you make a
mistake you are un-born again. They have **no
biblical substantiation**; it is nothing more than
religious superstition. When you become born
again, it is incorruptible seed. This seed is

stronger than the seed your father put in you, and **everything in God's Word states that it is seed, irrevocable** and permanently permanent. You may make mistakes in your flesh, but the spiritual seed of God cannot sin. The seed cannot be taken out of someone. This is grace; this is God's unconditional love.

When your children make mistakes, would you take your seed out of them if you could and cause them to die? Of course not. Neither would God. But you cannot take your seed out of your child, and God cannot take His seed out of His child because it is impossible for Him to break His Word.[*]

The last part of I Peter 1:23 states that you get born again by the Word of God. Well, exactly what is it in the Word of God that a man must believe to become born again of God's seed, of God's spirit? Observe carefully Peter ministering the new birth to people in Acts chapter 2.

---

[*]Numbers 23:19: **God is not a man, that he should lie; neither the son of man, that he should repent: hath he said, and shall he not do it? or hath he spoken, and shall he not make it good?**

Acts 2:22—24:

Ye men of Israel, hear these words; Jesus of Nazareth, a man approved of God among you by miracles and wonders and signs, which God did by him in the midst of you, as ye yourselves also know:

Him, being delivered by the determinate counsel and foreknowledge of God, ye have taken, and by wicked hands have crucified and slain:

Whom God hath raised up, having loosed the pains of death: because it was not possible that he should be holden of it.

First, Peter taught them that Jesus was a man. Then, in verse 23 he taught that Jesus Christ was crucified and killed.

We will see more of what you must believe to become born again of God's spirit in verse 36:

Therefore let all the house of Israel know assuredly, that God hath made that **same** Jesus, whom ye have crucified, **both Lord and Christ**.

This is not just any Jesus. This is the one who was crucified, **whom God raised from the dead**. And God has made him both lord and Christ. This same Jesus is Jesus Christ the lord. Peter taught that:

- Jesus was a man,
- he was crucified and killed,
- he is both lord and Christ, and
- **God raised him from the dead.**

Verses 37 and 38:
Now when they heard this, they were pricked in their heart, and said unto Peter and to the rest of the apostles, Men and brethren, what shall we do?

Then Peter said unto them, Repent, and be baptized every one of you **in the name of Jesus Christ** for the remission of sins, and ye shall receive the gift of the Holy Ghost [holy spirit].

They were pricked in their hearts and asked what they should do. He told them, "Repent and be baptized everyone of you in water." No he did not! He told them to be baptized in the name of Jesus Christ and that they would receive the gift of holy spirit, which is God's incorruptible seed, that third and most important part of man they were lacking.

Verse 47:
Praising God, and having favour with all the people. And the Lord added to the church daily such as should be saved.

"The Lord added to the church daily such as should be saved." "Saved" is the Greek word *sozo*, meaning to be made whole. This phrase should be translated: "as many as would be made whole." They were made whole because they had the third and most important part—the spiritual seed of God in them. You cannot see or touch spirit, but you can certainly learn how to utilize its power for joy, peace, and success.

The truths of receiving the new birth are spoken again in Acts chapter 4.

Acts 4:10 and 12:
Be it known unto you all, and to all the people of Israel, that by the **name of Jesus Christ** of Nazareth, whom ye **crucified**, whom **God raised from the dead**, even by him doth this man stand here before you whole.

Neither is there salvation in any other: for there is **none other name** under heaven given among men, whereby we **must be saved** [made whole].

Acts chapter 17 further illustrates this truth.

Acts 17:3 and 4:
Opening and alleging, that Christ must needs have **suffered**, and **risen** again from the **dead**; and that **this Jesus, whom I preach unto you, is Christ**.

And some of them believed, and consorted with Paul and Silas...

Here is the simplicity of what you must believe to be made whole, to become God's son, to receive the gift of holy spirit, the seed of God in you: that Jesus Christ suffered and died for you, that God raised **this** Jesus[*] from the dead, and that he is not any Jesus but Jesus the Christ. When you believe this, in an instant of time you will be born again, saved, a child of God with incorruptible seed.

Romans 10:9:
That if thou shalt confess with thy mouth the **Lord Jesus**, and shalt believe in thine heart that **God hath raised him from the dead**, thou shalt be saved.

---

[*]It is very important to distinguish him from all other Jesuses. He is Jesus Christ.

Verse 10:
For with the heart man believeth unto righteousness; and with the mouth confession is made unto salvation.

The word "Lord" is *kurios* in Greek. It means **anyone** who is in authority over another, including kings, masters, employers, God over all, and Jesus Christ over the Christians.

Here in Romans 10:9 and 10 is the simple how of becoming a Christian. **It is so very easy**; it only takes a few seconds to do. I have helped little children receive the gift of holy spirit, be born again. I have ministered the new birth to atheists. I have helped retarded people receive the new birth, holy spirit. I have helped people become born again of God's seed in their old age. The Word of God states "whosoever." The apostle who wrote this scripture in Romans was a religious fanatic who beat, murdered, and imprisoned Christians; and God in all His love and grace, made it available for him to be born again. This apostle Paul became the greatest of the apostles. You cannot deserve the new birth. You cannot earn it. It is a free gift of God's love to a person in need.

Putting Romans 10:9 and Acts together, you simply confess with your mouth that Jesus the Christ is your lord, and you believe that God has raised him from the dead.

- **You believe the man Jesus suffered and died the death of the crucifixion for you.**[*]
- **You believe God has raised him from the dead.**
- **You believe this Jesus is the Christ (the Son of God).**
- **You confess him as your lord.**

You are now God's son, His child born of incorruptible seed, a three-part whole man.

Now that you have the spirit of God permanently in you, you have the ability to study God's Word and learn all the principles to true success in every area of life, the capacity to study God's Word and unravel all the secrets and mysteries of life. I highly suggest you make an all-out effort to take the foundational class on *To Know God* in order to learn the keys to unfolding God's Word,[1] to operate the power to receive answers to your prayers,[2] and to learn the principles to fulfilling your heart's desires.[3]

---

[*] If you are new to the Bible, reading John chapters 18—21 would help you to understand what Jesus Christ accomplished for you.

The Belief

1. 1 Timothy 2:4:
   Who will have all men to be saved, and to
   come unto the knowledge of the truth.

2. Matthew 21:22:
   And all things, whatsoever ye shall ask in
   prayer, believing, ye shall receive.

3. Psalms 37:4:
   Delight thyself also in the LORD; and he shall
   give thee the desires of thine heart.

CHAPTER 9

How to Increase Your Trust in God

1. Focus on all the times you have trusted, believed, God. Consider them thoroughly and rejoice in them. This will encourage you to trust Him further.

Philippians 4:8:
Finally, brethren, whatsoever things are true, whatsoever things are honest, whatsoever things are just, whatsoever things are pure, whatsoever things are lovely, whatsoever things are of good report; if there be any virtue, and if there be any praise, think on these things.

2. The Word of God states that the flesh profits nothing.[*] God will never bless you because of your **works** or your **goodness**. All the promises of God are appropriated by your trust in Him; He blesses you because you trust Him. The battle of works versus believing is a mental battle you must consistently be cognizant of; for, the nature of man is to try to approach and please God by works (his own goodness), rather than to enjoy God and receive His goodness by believing.

> Romans 10:3 and 4:
> For they being ignorant of God's righteousness, and going about to establish their own righteousness, have not submitted themselves unto the righteousness of God.
>
> For Christ is the end of the law for righteousness to every one that believeth.

3. When you have failed to believe or trust God in a situation, do not allow yourself to be discouraged and certainly do not become negative about yourself. Make up your mind to learn to trust God and operate your spiritual power with vigor so next time you succeed!

---

[*]John 6:63: It is the spirit that quickeneth; the flesh profiteth nothing: the words that I speak unto you, they are spirit, and they are life.

All men fail to trust God at times; however, some people beat themselves down with their mistakes, causing many more mistakes.
(I John 3:20-22)

> Philippians 3:13:
> Brethren, I count not myself to have apprehended: but this one thing I do, forgetting those things which are behind, and reaching forth unto those things which are before,

4. Recognize temptation. Many times when it is difficult to be positive and trusting, you are being tempted and it is not your unbelief, but pressures from people, situations, and the **adversary**. Do not allow temptation to talk you out of success that is just around the corner.[*]

> I Peter 1:6 and 7:
> Wherein ye greatly rejoice, though now for a season, if need be, ye are in heaviness through manifold temptations:
>
> That the trial of your faith, being much more precious than of gold that perisheth, though it be tried with fire, might be found unto praise and honour and glory at the appearing of Jesus Christ:

---

*The name of Jesus Christ and the power of the holy spirit may be necessary to eliminate the temptation.

5.   When you are trusting God to correct a situation or to bring something to pass, there is often a genuine time element. For instance, when you are believing to have a baby, it will take at least nine months before the child is born. Be patient and steadfast in your trust.
   (I Corinthians 4:2, 15:58)

6. You can change quickly with God's help. It is very difficult to succeed or overcome fear without depending upon God's strength and love.

> Psalms 34:4:
> I sought the LORD, and he heard me, and delivered me from all my fears.

> II Corinthians 3:5:
> Not that we are sufficient of ourselves to think any thing as of ourselves; but our sufficiency is of God;

7. The greatest mistake is analyzing everything. You can analyze yourself out of believing anything.   Do not over-think your walk or situations; just pray about them and give them to God.

Proverbs 3:5 and 6:
Trust in the LORD with all thine heart; and lean not unto thine own understanding.

In all thy ways acknowledge him, and he shall direct thy paths.

8. The one-two punch for **sure success** is being (1) **adamantly positive** in your heart and (2) **very simple** on God's Word.
(II Corinthians 11:3)

9. **All strain is drain.** Cast your cares and travel light in your heart. You will never be able to understand everything.
(Deuteronomy 29:29, II Timothy 2:4)

I Peter 5:7:
Casting all your care upon him; for he careth for you.

10. Speaking and singing in tongues much causes you to have **fruit** in your life; believing is one of those fruits. Singing in tongues much can build you back up, **strengthen** you, **invigorate** you, and **encourage** you.
(Galatians 5:22, Ephesians 3:16, II Corinthians 4:16, Isaiah 28:11 and 12, I Corinthians 14.4)

11.   Study God's Word, not as an academic endeavor, but for **the purpose of sweet fellowship** with your Father, expecting that Word of God to deepen your trust.

> I Corinthians 2:4 and 5:
> And my speech and my preaching was not with enticing words of man's wisdom, but in demonstration of the Spirit and of power:
>
> That your faith should not stand in the wisdom of men, but in the power of God.

12.   The greatest key of all is to learn to walk in the love of God in renewed mind by watching your thoughts and bringing them back in harmony with God's Word, by putting thoughts of God's Word in your mind.   The practice of continuously discussing all you think and do with your loving friend and Father God is renewed mind love.   Love energizes believing.

> Galatians 5:6:
> For in Jesus Christ neither circumcision availeth any thing, nor uncircumcision; but faith which worketh by love.

> I Corinthians 13:8:
> Charity never faileth: [The love of God in your heart and mind **never** fails.]

13.   Fellowship with others who are moving ahead in their trust with God.

> Corrected translation of Romans 16.17:
> Now I lovingly ask you, family members, watch very carefully and mark those who cause dissension and divisions and set a trap alongside the doctrine which you have learned, and shun them and separate yourselves from them.

14.   Take the time to be **thankful**. This will heal your heart and encourage you greatly.

> Colossians 2:7:
> Rooted and built up in him, and stablished in the faith, as ye have been taught, abounding therein with thanksgiving.

15.   Recognize mental assent. Mental assent is when you confess positives with your mind or mouth, but in your heart you are really negative. Be honest with God, and work together with Him until your heart is positive.

16. Take action; be a doer of the Word. Become a decisive, action-oriented person (on the Word of God).

John 14:23:
Jesus answered and said unto him, If a man love me, **he will keep my words**: and my Father will love him, and we will come unto him, and make our abode with him.

James 1:22:
But be ye **doers** of the word, and not hearers only, deceiving your own selves.

17. **Honesty with God**
You will never go far with God in any area unless you develop an honest rapport with Him.

I John 1:8—10:
If we say that we have no sin, we deceive ourselves, and the truth is not in us.

If we confess our sins, he is faithful and just to forgive us our sins, and to **cleanse us from all unrighteousness.**

If we say that we have not sinned, we make him a liar, and his word is not in us.

18. Practice believing. Look for, find, and enjoy chances to believe God; step out on a few "limbs." We are to practice until we become masterful at trusting God.

19. Develop your partnership with God. Talk to Him about everything. And remember, you do your part; **do not try to do God's part for Him**.

Matthew 6:33:
But seek ye first the kingdom of God, and his righteousness; and all these things shall be added unto you.

Matthew 7:7 and 11:
Ask, and it shall be given you...

...how much more shall your Father which is in heaven give good things to them that ask him?

20. Once you have gone to God to the best of your ability and you still need help, go to a knowledgeable Christian brother or sister in whom you trust for assistance.

I Thessalonians 3:2:
And sent Timotheus, our brother, and minister of God, and our fellowlabourer in the gospel of Christ, to establish you, and to comfort you concerning your faith: